~IRISH~
PUB COOKING

pil

Publications International, Ltd.

Pictured on the front cover: Shepherd's Pie *(page 34)*.

Pictured on the back cover: *(clockwise from top left):* Pub-Style Fish & Chips *(page 92)*, Chocolate Stout Cake *(page 116)*, Irish Stout Chicken *(page 44)* and Mussels in Beer Broth *(page 96)*.

ISBN: 978-1-4508-9323-7

Library of Congress Control Number: 2012943995

Manufactured in China.

8 7 6 5 4 3 2 1

Microwave Cooking: Microwave ovens vary in wattage. Use the cooking times as guidelines and check for doneness before adding more time.

Preparation/Cooking Times: Preparation times are based on the approximate amount of time required to assemble the recipe before cooking, baking, chilling or serving. These times include preparation steps such as measuring, chopping and mixing. The fact that some preparations and cooking can be done simultaneously is taken into account. Preparation of optional ingredients and serving suggestions is not included.

While we hope this publication helps you find new ways to eat delicious foods, you may not always achieve the results desired due to variations in ingredients, cooking temperatures, typos, errors, omissions, or individual cooking abilities.

TABLE OF CONTENTS

Cranberry Scones
Makes 12 scones

1½ **cups all-purpose flour**
½ **cup oat bran**
¼ **cup plus 1 tablespoon sugar, divided**
2 **teaspoons baking powder**
½ **teaspoon baking soda**
½ **teaspoon salt**
¼ **cup plus 1 tablespoon cold butter**
¾ **cup dried cranberries**
⅓ **cup milk**
1 **egg**
¼ **cup sour cream**
1 **tablespoon old-fashioned or quick oats (optional)**

1. Preheat oven to 425°F.

2. Combine flour, oat bran, ¼ cup sugar, baking powder, baking soda and salt in large bowl; mix well. Cut in butter with pastry blender or two knives until mixture resembles coarse crumbs. Stir in cranberries.

3. Whisk milk and egg in small bowl until well blended. Reserve 2 tablespoons milk mixture. Stir sour cream into remaining milk mixture. Stir into flour mixture until soft dough forms.

4. Turn out dough onto floured surface. Gently knead 10 to 12 times. Shape dough into 9×6-inch rectangle. Cut dough into six 3-inch squares using floured knife; cut diagonally into halves, forming 12 triangles. Place 2 inches apart on ungreased baking sheets; brush with reserved milk mixture. Sprinkle with oats, if desired, and remaining 1 tablespoon sugar.

5. Bake 10 to 12 minutes or until golden brown. Remove to wire rack; cool 10 minutes. Serve warm.

Breakfast Hash

Makes 6 to 8 servings

**1 pound BOB EVANS® Special Seasonings or
   Savory Sage Roll Sausage**
2 cups chopped potatoes
¼ cup chopped red and/or green bell pepper
2 tablespoons chopped onion
6 eggs
2 tablespoons milk

Crumble sausage into large skillet. Add potatoes, pepper and onion. Cook over low heat until sausage is browned and potatoes are fork-tender, stirring occasionally. Drain off any drippings. Whisk eggs and milk in small bowl until blended. Add to sausage mixture; scramble until eggs are set but not dry. Serve hot. Refrigerate leftovers.

SERVING SUGGESTION: Serve with fresh fruit.

◆ Tip ◆

There's a lot more to potatoes than peeling them as any good Irish cook knows. The more than 4,000 different varieties of potatoes range in size from tiny fingerlings to huge baking potatoes and come in a rainbow of colors, including blue, yellow and purple. The three basic types are waxy, starchy and all-purpose. Starchy potatoes like Idaho bakers or russets are fluffy and absorbent. Waxy potatoes, like red-skinned potatoes, have a smoother, less starchy flesh that holds its shape better when cooked. All-purpose varieties, like Yukon Gold, are medium starch and will work in most any dish.

Breakfast Hash

Apple Cake
Makes 12 to 15 servings

1¼ cups granulated sugar, divided
1 cup (2 sticks) butter
¾ cup packed brown sugar
2 eggs
1 teaspoon vanilla
1 cup buttermilk
2½ cups all-purpose flour
2 teaspoons ground cinnamon, divided
1 teaspoon baking powder
1 teaspoon baking soda
1 teaspoon salt
¼ teaspoon ground nutmeg
3 cups chopped apples
1 cup chopped nuts

1. Preheat oven to 350°F. Grease 13×9-inch baking pan. Set aside.

2. Beat ¾ cup granulated sugar, butter, brown sugar, eggs and vanilla in large bowl with electric mixer at medium speed 3 minutes or until creamy. Beat in buttermilk.

3. Combine flour, 1 teaspoon cinnamon, baking powder, baking soda, salt and nutmeg in medium bowl. Beat into sugar mixture until well blended. Stir in apples.

4. Pour batter into prepared pan. Combine remaining ½ cup granulated sugar, remaining 1 teaspoon cinnamon and nuts in small bowl. Sprinkle over batter.

5. Bake 35 to 40 minutes or until toothpick inserted into center comes out clean. Cool completely on wire rack.

Apple Cake

Savory Cheddar Bread

Makes 16 slices

2 cups all-purpose flour
4 teaspoons baking powder
1 tablespoon sugar
½ teaspoon onion salt
½ teaspoon oregano, crushed
¼ teaspoon dry mustard
1 cup (4 ounces) SARGENTO® Fancy Shredded Mild or Sharp
  Cheddar Cheese
1 cup milk
1 egg, beaten
1 tablespoon butter or margarine, melted

In large bowl, stir together flour, baking powder, sugar, onion salt, oregano, dry mustard and cheese. In separate bowl, combine milk, egg and melted butter; add to dry ingredients, stirring just until moistened. Spread batter in greased 8×4-inch loaf pan. Bake at 350°F 45 minutes or until wooden pick inserted in center comes out clean. Cool 10 minutes on wire rack. Remove from pan.

Savory Cheddar Bread

Caramelized Bacon
Makes 6 servings

12 slices (about 12 ounces) applewood-smoked bacon
½ cup packed light brown sugar
2 tablespoons water
¼ to ½ teaspoon ground red pepper

1. Preheat oven to 375°F. Line 15×10-inch jelly-roll pan with heavy-duty foil. Spray wire rack with nonstick cooking spray; place in prepared pan.
2. Cut bacon in half crosswise, if desired; arrange in single layer on prepared wire rack. Combine brown sugar, water and red pepper in small bowl; mix well. Brush generously over surface of bacon.
3. Bake 20 to 25 minutes or until bacon is dark brown. Immediately transfer to serving platter; cool completely.

NOTE: Bacon can be prepared up to 3 days ahead and stored in the refrigerator between sheets of waxed paper in resealable food storage bag. Let stand at room temperature at least 30 minutes before serving.

Hash Brown Casserole with Bacon
Makes 12 servings

1 package (32 ounces) frozen southern-style hash brown
potatoes, thawed
1 container (16 ounces) sour cream
1 can (10¾ ounces) condensed cream of chicken soup, undiluted
1½ cups (6 ounces) shredded sharp Cheddar cheese
¾ cup thinly sliced green onions
4 slices bacon, crisp-cooked and crumbled
2 teaspoons hot pepper sauce
¼ teaspoon garlic salt

1. Preheat oven to 350°F. Spray 13×9-inch baking pan with nonstick cooking spray.
2. Combine potatoes, sour cream, soup, cheese, green onions, bacon, hot pepper sauce and garlic salt in large bowl. Spoon evenly into prepared dish.
3. Bake 55 to 60 minutes or until potatoes are tender and cooked through. Stir before serving.

Caramelized Bacon

Cinnamon Walnut Coffee Cake

Makes 12 to 16 servings

¾ cup chopped walnuts

1 teaspoon ground cinnamon

1¼ cups sugar

1 cup (2 sticks) butter, softened

2 eggs

1 cup sour cream

1⅓ cups all-purpose flour, plus more for dusting

⅓ cup CREAM OF WHEAT® Cinnamon Swirl Instant Hot Cereal, uncooked

1½ teaspoons baking powder

½ teaspoon baking soda

1 teaspoon vanilla extract

1. Coat Bundt® pan with nonstick cooking spray. Sprinkle lightly with flour; shake out any excess. Combine walnuts and cinnamon in small bowl; set aside.

2. Cream sugar, butter and eggs in mixing bowl with electric mixer at medium speed. Add sour cream; blend well. Add flour, Cream of Wheat, baking powder and baking soda; mix well. Stir in vanilla. Sprinkle half of walnut mixture into bottom of prepared Bundt pan. Evenly spread half of batter over mixture. Sprinkle remaining walnut mixture over batter. Top with remaining batter, spreading evenly in Bundt pan.

3. Set oven to 350°F (do not preheat); place Bundt pan in cold oven. Bake 45 minutes or until toothpick inserted near center comes out clean. Remove from oven; let stand 5 minutes. Place serving plate over Bundt pan and turn pan over carefully onto plate; remove pan. Serve cake warm or cool.

TIP: You can also bake this cake in regular square or round cake pans. Divide the batter between two 8- or 9-inch pans and sprinkle each with one-half of walnut mixture. Bake 25 to 30 minutes.

PREP TIME: 15 minutes

START TO FINISH TIME: 1 hour

Broccoli, Potato & Bacon Egg Pie with Cheddar Cheese

Makes 6 to 8 servings

2 cups cooked broccoli florets

1½ cups cooked diced potatoes (about 2 medium)

1½ cups (lightly packed) grated **CABOT®** Sharp Cheddar Cheese (about 4 ounces)

4 slices cooked bacon, chopped

1 unbaked 9-inch deep-dish or 10-inch pie shell

6 large eggs

2 large egg yolks

1½ cups heavy cream

1 teaspoon mild paprika

½ teaspoon salt

¼ teaspoon freshly ground black pepper

1. Preheat oven to 350°F.

2. Distribute broccoli, potatoes, cheese and bacon evenly in pie shell. In mixing bowl, whisk together whole eggs and egg yolks until well combined; add cream, paprika, salt and pepper and whisk again.

3. Pour cream mixture evenly over ingredients in pie shell. Bake for 30 to 40 minutes, or until golden on top and set all the way to center.

Raisin Oat Scones

Makes 30 scones

2 cups all-purpose flour
2 teaspoons baking powder
½ teaspoon baking soda
¼ teaspoon salt
1 cup old-fashioned oats
½ cup cold butter, cut into pieces
1 cup raisins
1 cup buttermilk

1. Preheat oven to 425°F. Grease baking sheet.

2. Sift flour, baking powder, baking soda and salt into medium bowl. Stir in oats. Using pastry blender or two knives, cut in butter until mixture resembles coarse crumbs. Add raisins. Stir in enough buttermilk to make soft dough.

3. Turn out dough onto lightly floured surface; knead until smooth. Roll out dough to 12×10-inch rectangle. Cut into 2-inch squares.

4. Arrange scones on prepared baking sheet. Bake about 15 minutes or until browned.

 Tip ◆

Scones originated somewhere in the British Isles centuries ago. It's unclear precisely where, but one legend says the name came from the Stone (or scone) of Destiny, where Scottish kings were once crowned. Scones can be savory or sweet and are served for breakfast or tea.

Raisin Oat Scones

Sunrise Sausage Bake
Makes 12 servings

**2 cans (12 fluid ounces *each*) NESTLÉ® CARNATION®
  Evaporated Milk**
8 large eggs, beaten
1 pound precooked sausage links, cut into ¼-inch slices
2 cups (8-ounce package) shredded Cheddar cheese
1 cup chopped red and/or green bell pepper
2 green onions (green parts only), sliced
½ teaspoon onion powder
¼ teaspoon garlic powder
8 cups ½-inch cubed Italian or French bread (about 9 slices)

PREHEAT oven to 350°F. Grease 13×9-inch baking dish.

COMBINE evaporated milk, eggs, sausage, cheese, red pepper, green onions, onion powder and garlic powder in large bowl. Add bread cubes, stirring gently to moisten bread. Pour mixture into baking dish.

BAKE for 45 minutes or until set. Serve warm.

TIP: This bake can be assembled ahead of time and refrigerated. Let stand at room temperature for 30 minutes before baking.

TIP: Substitute multi-grain bread for Italian or French bread.

PREP TIME: 20 minutes
BAKING TIME: 45 minutes

Sunrise Sausage Bake

Oatmeal with Apples and Cottage Cheese
Makes 2 servings

½ cup uncooked old-fashioned oats
½ cup diced apple
⅔ cup water
½ cup cottage cheese
¾ teaspoon ground cinnamon
1 teaspoon vanilla
   Dash salt
¼ cup half-and-half
2 tablespoons chopped pecans or almonds
1½ tablespoons sugar

Combine oats, apple, water, cottage cheese, cinnamon, vanilla and salt in large microwaveable bowl; stir. Cover and vent. Microwave on HIGH 2 minutes; let stand 2 minutes. Stir in half-and-half, pecans and sugar.

◆ Tip ◆

Old-fashioned or rolled oats are steamed and flattened with huge rollers so they cook quickly. Steel-cut or Irish oats are cut into pieces but not rolled. They take considerably longer to cook and have a different, chewier texture that many people enjoy. To substitute steel-cut oats in this recipe, consult the cooking times on the label. Fortunately, oats retain their nutrients whether or not they are rolled.

Oatmeal with Apples and Cottage Cheese

Egg & Sausage Casserole

Makes 6 servings

8 ounces bulk pork sausage
3 tablespoons butter, divided
2 tablespoons all-purpose flour
¼ teaspoon salt
¼ teaspoon black pepper
1¼ cups milk
2 cups frozen hash brown potatoes, thawed
4 eggs, hard-cooked and sliced
½ cup cornflake crumbs
¼ cup sliced green onions

1. Preheat oven to 350°F. Spray 2-quart baking dish with nonstick cooking spray.

2. Brown sausage in large skillet over medium-high heat 6 to 8 minutes, stirring to break up meat. Drain fat. Transfer to plate.

3. Melt 2 tablespoons butter in same skillet over medium heat. Stir in flour, salt and pepper until smooth. Gradually stir in milk; cook and stir until thickened. Add sausage, potatoes and eggs; stir until blended. Transfer to prepared baking dish.

4. Melt remaining 1 tablespoon butter in small saucepan over low heat. Add cornflake crumbs; stir until combined. Sprinkle evenly over casserole.

5. Bake 30 minutes or until hot and bubbly. Sprinkle with green onions just before serving.

Egg & Sausage Casserole

Bacon-Cheddar Muffins
Makes 12 muffins

2 cups all-purpose flour
¾ cup sugar
2 teaspoons baking powder
½ teaspoon baking soda
½ teaspoon salt
¾ cup plus 2 tablespoons milk
⅓ cup butter, melted and slightly cooled
1 egg
1 cup (4 ounces) shredded Cheddar cheese
6 slices bacon, crisp-cooked and crumbled

1. Preheat oven to 350°F. Grease 12 standard (2½-inch) muffin cups.

2. Combine flour, sugar, baking powder, baking soda and salt in medium bowl. Combine milk, butter and egg in small bowl; mix well. Add milk mixture to flour mixture; stir until blended. Gently stir in cheese and bacon. Spoon batter into prepared muffin cups, filling three-fourths full.

3. Bake 15 to 20 minutes or until toothpick inserted into centers comes out clean. Cool in pan 2 minutes; remove to wire rack. Serve warm or at room temperature.

Bacon-Cheddar Muffins

COUNTRY CLASSICS

Smoked Sausage and Cabbage
Makes 4 servings

1 pound smoked sausage, cut into 2-inch pieces
1 tablespoon olive oil
6 cups coarsely chopped cabbage
1 yellow onion, cut into ½-inch wedges
2 cloves garlic, minced
¾ teaspoon sugar
¼ teaspoon caraway seeds
¼ teaspoon salt
¼ teaspoon black pepper
   Hot mashed potatoes

1. Heat large nonstick skillet over medium-high heat. Add sausage; cook and stir 3 minutes or until browned. Transfer to plate.

2. Heat oil in same skillet. Add cabbage, onion, garlic, sugar, caraway seeds, salt and pepper; cook and stir 5 minutes or until onion begins to brown. Add sausage; cover and cook 5 minutes. Remove from heat. Let stand 5 minutes. Serve sausage mixture over mashed potatoes.

Beef Pot Pie

Makes 4 to 6 servings

½ cup all-purpose flour
1 teaspoon salt, divided
½ teaspoon black pepper, divided
1½ pounds beef stew meat
2 tablespoons olive oil
1 pound new red potatoes, cut into bite-size pieces
2 cups baby carrots
1 cup frozen pearl onions, thawed
1 parsnip, peeled and cut into 1-inch pieces
1½ cups Irish stout
1 cup beef broth
1 teaspoon chopped fresh thyme *or* ½ teaspoon dried thyme
½ (about 15-ounce) package refrigerated pie crust (1 crust)

1. Preheat oven to 350°F. Combine flour, ½ teaspoon salt and ¼ teaspoon pepper in large resealable food storage bag. Add beef and shake to coat.

2. Heat oil in large skillet over medium-high heat. Add beef in batches and brown on both sides, turning once. Do not crowd meat. Transfer to 2½- to 3-quart casserole. Add potatoes, carrots, onions and parsnip; mix well.

3. Add stout, broth, thyme, remaining ½ teaspoon salt and ¼ teaspoon pepper to same skillet. Bring to a boil, scraping up browned bits from bottom of skillet. Pour into casserole.

4. Cover; bake 2½ to 3 hours or until meat is fork-tender, stirring once. Remove cover. Let stand at room temperature 15 minutes.

5. *Increase oven temperature to 425°F.* Soften pie crust as directed on package. Place over casserole and press edges to seal. Cut slits in crust to vent. Bake 15 to 20 minutes or until crust is golden brown. Cool slightly before serving.

INDIVIDUAL BEEF POT PIES: Instead of refrigerated pie crust, use half of a 17-ounce package of puff pastry. Divide beef filling among ovenproof individual serving dishes. Cut puff pastry to fit; press over moistened edges and crimp to seal. Brush tops with 1 lightly beaten egg yolk. Bake in preheated 400°F oven 15 to 20 minutes or until crust is puffed and golden.

Beef Pot Pie

Bacon-Roasted Brussels Sprouts

Makes 4 servings

1 pound brussels sprouts
3 slices bacon, cut into ½-inch pieces
2 teaspoons brown sugar
   Salt and black pepper

1. Preheat oven to 400°F. Trim ends from brussels sprouts; cut in half lengthwise.

2. Combine brussels sprouts, bacon and brown sugar in baking dish.

3. Roast 25 to 30 minutes or until golden brown, stirring once. Season with salt and pepper.

Parsnip Patties

Makes 4 patties

  1 pound parsnips, peeled and cut into ¾-inch chunks
  4 tablespoons (½ stick) butter, divided
  ¼ cup chopped onion
  ¼ cup all-purpose flour
  ⅓ cup milk
  2 teaspoons chopped fresh chives
    Salt and black pepper
  ¾ cup fresh bread crumbs
  2 tablespoons vegetable oil

1. Pour 1 inch water into medium saucepan. Bring to a boil over high heat. Add parsnips; cover and cook 10 minutes or until fork-tender. Drain. Place in large bowl. Coarsely mash with fork.

2. Melt 2 tablespoons butter in small skillet over medium-high heat. Add onion; cook and stir until transparent. Whisk in flour until bubbly and lightly browned. Whisk in milk until thickened. Stir flour mixture into mashed parsnips. Stir in chives; season with salt and pepper.

3. Form parsnip mixture into four patties. Spread bread crumbs on plate. Dip patties in bread crumbs to coat all sides evenly. Place on waxed paper and refrigerate 2 hours.

4. Melt remaining 2 tablespoons butter and oil in large skillet over medium-high heat. Add patties; cook 5 minutes per side or until browned.

Bacon-Roasted Brussels Sprouts

Cabbage Rolls

Makes 4 servings

1 pound ground beef
1 can (8 ounces) tomato sauce, divided
⅔ cup chopped onion, divided
½ cup uncooked rice
2 cloves garlic, minced, divided
1 teaspoon salt, divided
½ teaspoon black pepper, divided
8 cabbage leaves
1 teaspoon vegetable oil
1 cup thinly sliced cabbage
1 can (about 14 ounces) diced tomatoes
2 bay leaves
⅓ cup raisins

1. Bring 3 quarts water to a boil in Dutch oven.

2. Meanwhile, combine beef, 2 tablespoons tomato sauce, ⅓ cup onion, rice, half of garlic, ¾ teaspoon salt and ¼ teaspoon pepper in medium bowl; mix until well blended.

3. Place cabbage leaves in boiling water in two batches. Cook 1 minute or until softened. Drain in colander; let stand until cool enough to handle. Cut out thick stem of each leaf with small sharp knife. Place one eighth of beef mixture on each leaf near stem end. Roll up, folding in sides. Repeat with remaining leaves and filling.

4. Heat oil in large skillet over medium heat. Add remaining ⅓ cup onion; cook and stir 2 minutes. Add sliced cabbage; cook and stir about 3 minutes or until slightly wilted. Add tomatoes, remaining tomato sauce, bay leaves, remaining garlic, ¼ teaspoon salt and ¼ teaspoon pepper. Bring to a boil. Stir in raisins.

5. Arrange cabbage rolls in skillet. Reduce heat. Cover and simmer about 1 hour. Remove and discard bay leaves. Serve cabbage rolls with sauce.

Cabbage Rolls

Shepherd's Pie

Makes 4 servings

1⅓ cups instant mashed potato flakes
1⅔ cups milk
2 tablespoons butter
1 teaspoon salt, divided
1 pound ground beef
¼ teaspoon black pepper
1 jar (12 ounces) beef gravy
1 package (10 ounces) frozen mixed vegetables, thawed and
   drained
¾ cup grated Parmesan cheese

1. Preheat broiler. Prepare 4 servings of mashed potatoes according to package directions, using milk, butter and ½ teaspoon salt.

2. Meanwhile, brown beef in large broilerproof skillet over medium-high heat, stirring to break up meat. Drain fat. Sprinkle beef with remaining ½ teaspoon salt and pepper. Add gravy and vegetables; mix well. Cook over medium-low heat 5 minutes or until heated through.

3. Spoon prepared potatoes around outside edge of skillet, leaving 3-inch circle in center. Sprinkle cheese evenly over potatoes. Broil 4 to 5 inches from heat 3 minutes or until cheese is golden brown and beef mixture is bubbly.

PREP AND COOK TIME: 28 minutes

Shepherd's Pie

Dublin Coddle One-Dish Dinner

Makes 4 servings

3 slices uncooked bacon, cut into small pieces
6 frozen pork sausage links, cut in half crosswise*
1 cup thinly sliced onion
1 cup ¼-inch-thick sliced carrots
1 packages SIMPLY POTATOES® Homestyle Slices
1 cup apple juice
1 tablespoon parsley
½ teaspoon salt

*If sausages are too frozen to cut, thaw slightly.

1. In 4-quart Dutch oven or large saucepan, cook bacon and sausage links until browned. Drain on paper towels; set aside.

2. In same saucepan cook onion, stirring occasionally, or until soft and lightly golden. Add carrots, SIMPLY POTATOES®, apple juice, parsley, salt and cooked bacon and sausage links.

3. Reduce heat to low. Cover; cook 30 to 35 minutes or until potatoes and vegetables are soft, adding more apple juice if mixture gets too dry.

PREP TIME: 15 minutes
COOK TIME: 35 minutes
TOTAL TIME: 50 minutes

◆ Tip ◆

Add some spice and heat to this entrée by using
spicy pork sausage links.

Irish Lamb Stew

Makes 8 servings

½ cup all-purpose flour
2 teaspoons salt, divided
½ teaspoon pepper, divided
3 pounds boneless lamb stew meat, cut into 1½-inch cubes
3 tablespoons vegetable oil
1 cup chopped onion
1 can (about 15 ounces) Irish stout
1 teaspoon sugar
1 teaspoon dried thyme
1 pound small new potatoes, quartered
1 pound carrots, peeled and cut into ½-inch pieces
½ cup water
1 cup frozen peas
¼ cup chopped fresh parsley

1. Mix flour with 1 teaspoon salt and ¼ teaspoon pepper in large bowl. Toss lamb in flour mixture and shake off excess; discard leftover flour. Heat oil in Dutch oven over medium heat. Brown lamb on all sides in batches, about 7 minutes per batch. Transfer to bowl.

2. Add onion and ¼ cup stout to Dutch oven; cook over medium heat 10 minutes, scraping up any browned bits. Return lamb to Dutch oven and stir in remaining stout, sugar, thyme, remaining 1 teaspoon salt and ¼ teaspoon pepper. Add water so that liquid just covers lamb, if needed. Cover; simmer 1½ hours or until lamb is tender.

3. Add potatoes, carrots and ½ cup water. Cook, covered, 30 minutes or until vegetables are tender. Stir in peas and parsley; simmer 5 to 10 minutes or until heated through.

Cabbage Colcannon

Makes 6 side-dish servings

1 pound new red potatoes, halved
1 tablespoon vegetable oil
1 small onion, thinly sliced
½ small head green cabbage, thinly sliced
  Salt and black pepper
3 tablespoons salted butter, divided

1. Place potatoes and enough water to cover in medium saucepan. Bring to a boil. Cook 20 minutes or until tender. Drain well.

2. Heat oil in large nonstick skillet over medium-high heat. Add onion; cook and stir 8 minutes or until onion is lightly browned. Add cabbage; cook and stir 5 minutes or until softened.

3. Add potatoes to skillet; cook until heated through. Slightly mash potatoes. Season to taste with salt and pepper. Place ½ tablespoon of butter on each portion just before serving.

Potato-Cauliflower Mash

Makes 4 (½-cup) servings

3 cups water
2 cups cubed unpeeled Yukon Gold potatoes (about 12 ounces)
10 ounces frozen cauliflower florets
¼ cup evaporated milk
2 tablespoons butter
¾ teaspoon salt
¼ teaspoon black pepper

1. Bring water to a boil in large saucepan. Add potatoes and cauliflower; return to a boil. Reduce heat; cover and simmer 10 minutes or until potatoes are tender.

2. Drain vegetables; place in blender with evaporated milk, butter, salt and pepper. Blend until smooth, scraping side frequently.

Cabbage Colcannon

Irish Soda Bread Rounds

Makes 8 rounds

4 cups all-purpose flour
¼ cup sugar
1 tablespoon baking powder
1 teaspoon baking soda
1 teaspoon salt
⅓ cup shortening
1 cup currants or raisins
1¾ cups buttermilk
1 egg

1. Preheat oven to 350°F. Grease two baking sheets; set aside.

2. Sift flour, sugar, baking powder, baking soda and salt into large bowl. Cut in shortening with pastry blender or two knives until mixture resembles coarse crumbs. Stir in currants. Beat buttermilk and egg in medium bowl until well blended. Add buttermilk mixture to flour mixture; stir until mixture forms soft dough.

3. Turn out dough onto floured surface; knead 10 to 12 times. Shape dough into 8 rounds; place on prepared baking sheets. Score top of each round with tip of sharp knife, making an X about 1 inch long and ¼ inch deep.

4. Bake 25 to 28 minutes or until toothpick inserted into centers comes out clean. Immediately remove from baking sheets; cool on wire racks.*

For a sweet crust, combine 1 tablespoon sugar and 1 tablespoon water in small bowl; brush over hot bread.

Irish Soda Bread Rounds

Rack of Lamb
Makes 4 servings

2 tablespoons chopped fresh parsley
2 tablespoons chopped fresh thyme
2 tablespoons Dijon mustard
½ cup Irish stout
1 rack of lamb, well-trimmed
½ teaspoon kosher salt
½ teaspoon black pepper

1. Preheat oven to 400°F. Spray broiler pan and rack with nonstick cooking spray.

2. Combine parsley, thyme and mustard in small bowl; whisk in stout.

3. Sprinkle both sides of lamb with salt and pepper; spread with stout mixture. Place lamb, bone side down, on prepared broiler pan; place pan on center oven rack. Bake 45 minutes to 145°F for medium-rare or desired doneness. Cover with foil; let stand 10 minutes before serving. Slice into 8 pieces.

 Tip ◆

To help prevent too much browning on the tips of
the bones, cover them with aluminum foil.

Rack of Lamb

Irish Stout Chicken
Makes 4 servings

2 tablespoons vegetable oil, divided
1 whole chicken (3 to 4 pounds), cut into serving pieces
1 medium onion, chopped
2 cloves garlic, minced
5 carrots, chopped
2 parsnips, peeled and chopped
1 teaspoon dried thyme
¾ teaspoon salt
½ teaspoon black pepper
¾ cup Irish stout
½ pound mushrooms
¾ cup frozen peas

1. Heat oil in large skillet over medium heat. Add chicken in single layer in skillet; cook over medium-high heat 5 minutes per side or until lightly browned. Transfer chicken to plate.

2. Add onion and garlic to drippings in skillet; cook and stir 3 minutes or until tender.

3. Return chicken and any accumulated juices to skillet with carrots, parsnips, thyme, salt and pepper. Pour stout over chicken and vegetables. Bring to a boil over high heat. Reduce heat to low. Cover and simmer 35 minutes.

4. Add mushrooms and peas to skillet. Cover and cook 10 minutes.

5. Uncover skillet; increase heat to medium. Cook 10 minutes or until sauce is slightly reduced and chicken is cooked through (165°F).

Irish Stout Chicken

Corned Beef & Cabbage
with Horseradish Mustard Sauce
Makes 6 to 8 servings

1 large onion, cut into chunks
1½ cups baby carrots
16 small red potatoes (about 1¼ pounds), cut into bite-size pieces
1 corned beef brisket (2 to 2½ pounds)
½ large head cabbage (1 pound), cut into 8 thin wedges
⅓ cup sour cream
⅓ cup mayonnaise
2 tablespoons Dijon mustard
2 tablespoons prepared horseradish

SLOW COOKER DIRECTIONS

1. Coat slow cooker with nonstick cooking spray. Place onion, carrots and potatoes in bottom of 4- to 5-quart slow cooker. Drain corned beef, reserving spice packet and juices from package. Place corned beef over vegetables; pour juices over beef and top with contents of spice packet. Add enough water to barely cover beef and vegetables (about 4 cups). Cover; cook on LOW 8 to 9 hours or on HIGH 5 to 6 hours or until corned beef is fork-tender.

2. Transfer corned beef to large sheet of heavy-duty foil; wrap tightly and set aside. Add cabbage wedges to vegetables, pushing down into liquid. Increase heat to HIGH. Cover; cook on HIGH 30 to 40 minutes or until vegetables are tender.

3. Meanwhile, combine sour cream, mayonnaise, mustard and horseradish; mix well. Reserve ½ cup of juices in slow cooker. Drain vegetables; transfer to serving platter. Thinly slice corned beef; arrange on platter and drizzle with reserved juices. Serve with horseradish mustard sauce.

Corned Beef & Cabbage with Horseradish Mustard Sauce

~ BREADS & ~ BOWLS

Celtic Knots
Makes 16 knots

1 package (16 ounces) hot roll mix, plus ingredients to prepare mix
1 egg white
2 teaspoons water
2 tablespoons coarse salt

1. Prepare hot roll mix according to package directions.

2. Preheat oven to 375°F. Lightly grease baking sheets.

3. Divide dough into 16 pieces; shape each piece into 10- to 12-inch rope. Form each rope into interlocking rings as shown in photo; place on prepared baking sheets. Moisten ends of rope at seams; pinch to seal.

4. Beat egg white and water in small bowl until foamy. Brush mixture onto dough; sprinkle with salt.

5. Bake about 15 minutes or until golden brown. Serve warm or at room temperature.

 **Tip**

For additional flavor, try different seasonings on the knots instead of salt. Sprinkle them lightly with black pepper or garlic powder and grated Parmesan cheese, poppy seeds or sesame seeds before baking.

Ham, Potato & Cabbage Soup
Makes 6 servings

1 tablespoon vegetable oil
2 large onions, chopped (about 2 cups)
1 clove garlic, minced
6 cups SWANSON® Chicken Broth (Regular, Natural Goodness®
    or Certified Organic)
¼ teaspoon ground black pepper
3 cups shredded cabbage
1 large potato, diced (about 2 cups)
½ of an 8-ounce cooked ham steak, cut into 2-inch-long strips
    (about 1 cup)
2 tablespoons chopped fresh parsley
1 teaspoon caraway seeds (optional)

1. Heat the oil in a 6-quart saucepot over medium-high heat. Add the onions and garlic and cook for 3 minutes or until tender, stirring occasionally.

2. Stir the broth, black pepper, cabbage, potato and ham in the saucepot and heat to a boil. Reduce the heat to low. Cover and cook for 30 minutes or until the potato is tender.

3. Stir in the parsley and caraway seeds, if desired.

KITCHEN TIP: A small head of cabbage, about 1 pound, will be enough for the amount of cabbage needed for this soup.

PREP TIME: 30 minutes
COOK TIME: 40 minutes

Ham, Potato & Cabbage Soup

Irish-Style Scones
Makes 6 scones

   3 eggs, divided
 ½ cup whipping cream
1½ teaspoons vanilla
   2 cups all-purpose flour
   2 teaspoons baking powder
 ¼ teaspoon salt
 ¼ cup (½ stick) cold butter
 ¼ cup finely chopped pitted dates
 ¼ cup golden raisins or currants
   1 teaspoon water
      Orange marmalade
      Softly whipped cream

1. Preheat oven to 375°F. Lightly grease large baking sheet; set aside. Beat 2 eggs, cream and vanilla in medium bowl; set aside.

2. Combine flour, baking powder and salt in medium bowl. Cut in butter with pastry blender or two knives until mixture resembles coarse crumbs. Stir in dates and raisins. Add cream mixture; mix just until moistened.

3. With floured hands, knead dough four times on lightly floured surface. Place dough on prepared cookie sheet; pat into 8-inch circle. With sharp wet knife, gently score dough into six wedges, cutting ¾ of the way into dough. Beat remaining egg with water; brush lightly over dough.

4. Bake 18 to 20 minutes or until golden brown. Cool 5 minutes on wire rack. Cut into wedges. Serve warm with marmalade and whipped cream.

Irish-Style Scones

Oxtail Soup with Beer
Makes 4 servings

2½ pounds oxtails (beef or veal)
1 large onion, sliced
4 carrots, cut into 1-inch pieces, divided
3 stalks celery, cut into 1-inch pieces, divided
2 sprigs fresh parsley
5 whole black peppercorns
1 bay leaf
4 cups beef broth
8 ounces Irish stout or porter
2 cups diced baking potatoes
1 teaspoon salt
Chopped fresh parsley (optional)

1. Combine oxtails, onion, half of carrots, one third of celery, 2 sprigs parsley, peppercorns and bay leaf in large saucepan. Pour broth and stout over mixture; bring to a boil. Reduce heat to low; simmer, covered, 3 hours or until meat is falling off bones.

2. Remove oxtails and set aside. Strain broth and return to saucepan; skim fat. Add remaining carrots, celery and potatoes; bring to a simmer. Cook 10 to 15 minutes or until vegetables are tender.

3. Remove meat from oxtails and return meat to saucepan. Stir in salt and heat through. Ladle soup into bowls and garnish with chopped parsley.

Oxtail Soup with Beer

Quaker's Best Oatmeal Bread
Makes 2 loaves (32 servings)

5¾ to 6¼ cups all-purpose flour
2½ cups QUAKER® Oats (quick or old fashioned, uncooked)
¼ cup granulated sugar
2 packages (¼ ounce each) quick-rising yeast
   (about 4½ teaspoons)
2½ teaspoons salt
1½ cups water
1¼ cups fat-free (skim) milk
¼ cup (½ stick) margarine or butter

1. Combine 3 cups flour, oats, sugar, yeast and salt in large bowl; mix well. Heat water, milk and margarine in small saucepan until very warm (120°F to 130°F). Add to flour mixture. Blend with electric mixer at low speed until dry ingredients are moistened. Increase to medium speed; beat 3 minutes. By hand, gradually stir in enough remaining flour to make stiff dough.

2. Turn dough out onto lightly floured surface. Knead 5 to 8 minutes or until smooth and elastic. Shape dough into ball; place in greased bowl, turning once. Cover; let rise in warm place 30 minutes or until doubled in size.

3. Punch down dough. Cover; let rest 10 minutes. Divide dough in half; shape to form loaves. Place in two greased 8×4-inch or 9×5-inch loaf pans. Cover; let rise in warm place 15 minutes or until nearly doubled in size.

4. Heat oven to 375°F. Bake 45 to 50 minutes or until dark golden brown. Remove from pans to wire rack. Cool completely before slicing.

◆ Tip ◆

If desired, brush tops of loaves lightly with melted margarine or butter and sprinkle with additional oats after placing in pans.

Quaker's Best Oatmeal Bread

Irish Stew in Bread
Makes 6 to 8 servings

1½ pounds lean, boned American lamb shoulder, cut into 1-inch
    cubes
¼ cup all-purpose flour
2 tablespoons vegetable oil
2 cloves garlic, crushed
2 cups water
¼ cup Burgundy wine
5 medium carrots, chopped
3 medium potatoes, peeled and sliced
2 large onions, peeled and chopped
2 ribs celery, sliced
¾ teaspoon black pepper
1 cube beef bouillon, crushed
1 cup frozen peas
¼ pound sliced fresh mushrooms
    Round bread, unsliced*

Stew can be served individually in small loaves or in one large loaf. Slice bread crosswise near top to form lid. Hollow larger piece, leaving 1-inch border. Fill "bowl" with hot stew; cover with "lid." Serve immediately.

Coat lamb with flour while heating oil in Dutch oven over low heat. Add lamb and garlic; cook and stir until brown. Add water, wine, carrots, potatoes, onions, celery, pepper and bouillon. Cover; simmer 30 to 35 minutes.

Add peas and mushrooms. Cover; simmer 10 minutes. Bring to a boil; adjust seasonings, if necessary. Serve in bread.

Favorite recipe from AMERICAN LAMB BOARD

Country Buttermilk Biscuits
Makes about 9 biscuits

2 cups all-purpose flour
1 tablespoon baking powder
2 teaspoons sugar
½ teaspoon salt
½ teaspoon baking soda
⅓ cup shortening
⅔ cup buttermilk*

*Or substitute soured fresh milk. To sour milk, combine 2½ teaspoons lemon juice plus enough milk to equal ⅔ cup. Stir; let stand 5 minutes before using.

1. Preheat oven to 450°F.

2. Combine flour, baking powder, sugar, salt and baking soda in medium bowl. Cut in shortening with pastry blender or two knives until mixture resembles coarse crumbs. Make well in center of dry ingredients. Add buttermilk; stir until mixture forms soft dough.

3. Turn out dough onto well-floured surface. Knead dough gently 10 to 12 times. Roll or pat dough to ½-inch thickness. Cut biscuits with floured 2½-inch biscuit cutter. Place 2 inches apart on ungreased baking sheet. Bake 8 to 10 minutes or until golden brown. Serve warm.

DROP BISCUITS: Prepare Country Buttermilk Biscuits as directed in steps 1 and 2, except increase buttermilk to 1 cup. After adding buttermilk, stir batter with wooden spoon about 15 strokes. Do not knead. Drop dough by heaping tablespoonfuls 1 inch apart onto greased baking sheets. Bake as directed in step 4. Makes about 18 biscuits.

SOUR CREAM DILL BISCUITS: Prepare Country Buttermilk Biscuits as directed in steps 1 and 2, except omit buttermilk. Combine ½ cup sour cream, ⅓ cup milk and 1 tablespoon chopped fresh dill or 1 teaspoon dried dill weed in small bowl until well blended. Stir into dry ingredients and continue as directed in steps 3 and 4. Makes about 9 biscuits.

BACON 'N' ONION BISCUITS: Prepare Country Buttermilk Biscuits as directed in steps 1 and 2, except add 4 slices crumbled crisply cooked bacon (about ⅓ cup) and ⅓ cup chopped green onions before adding buttermilk. Continue as directed in steps 3 and 4. Makes about 9 biscuits.

Sweet and Sour Cabbage Soup
Makes 8 to 10 servings

2 pounds boneless beef chuck roast
  Nonstick cooking spray
1 can (about 28 ounces) tomatoes, cut into pieces, undrained
1 can (about 15 ounces) tomato sauce
1 large onion, thinly sliced
3 carrots, shredded
2 pounds green cabbage, shredded
4 cups water
¾ cup sugar
½ cup lemon juice
1 tablespoon caraway seeds
2 teaspoons salt
1 teaspoon black pepper

SLOW COOKER DIRECTIONS

1. Cut beef into 4 pieces. Spray 12-inch skillet with cooking spray; heat over medium-high heat. Brown meat on all sides; transfer to slow cooker. Layer tomatoes, tomato sauce, onion, carrots, cabbage, water, sugar and lemon juice over beef. Sprinkle with caraway seeds, salt and pepper. Cover; cook on LOW 6 to 8 hours.

2. Remove beef from slow cooker. Shred beef and return to slow cooker; mix well.

◆ Tip ◆

Cabbage is a favorite vegetable in Irish cooking. Look
for green or red cabbage with tightly packed leaves and
compact heads. Discard outer leaves if they are loose or
limp. To shred cabbage, cut the head in half on a large
cutting board and cut out the hard core. Holding the
cabbage at slight angle use a large, sharp knife to thinly
slice it into long thin strands.

Sweet and Sour Cabbage Soup

Sausage and Cheddar Corn Bread

Makes 10 servings

1 tablespoon vegetable oil
½ pound bulk pork sausage
1 medium onion, chopped
1 jalapeño pepper,* minced
1 package (8 ounces) corn muffin mix
1 cup (4 ounces) shredded Cheddar cheese, divided
⅓ cup milk
1 egg

*Jalapeño peppers can sting and irritate the skin, so wear rubber gloves when handling peppers and do not touch your eyes.

1. Heat oil in large cast iron skillet over medium heat. Brown sausage, stirring to break up meat. Add onion and jalapeño; cook and stir 5 minutes or until softened. Remove sausage mixture to medium bowl.

2. Preheat oven to 350°F. Combine corn muffin mix, ½ cup cheese, milk and egg in separate medium bowl. Pour batter into skillet. Spread sausage mixture over top. Sprinkle with remaining ½ cup cheese.

3. Bake 20 to 25 minutes or until edges are lightly browned. Cut into wedges. Refrigerate leftovers.

PREP TIME: 15 minutes
COOK TIME: 20 minutes

Sausage and Cheddar Cornbread

Creamy Irish Potato Soup
Makes 5 servings

2 tablespoons butter
4 medium green onions, sliced (about ½ cup)
1 stalk celery, sliced (about ½ cup)
**1¾ cups SWANSON® Chicken Broth (Regular, Natural Goodness®
    or Certified Organic)**
⅛ teaspoon ground black pepper
3 medium potatoes, sliced ¼-inch thick (about 3 cups)
1½ cups milk

1. Heat the butter in a 3-quart saucepan over medium heat. Add the onions and celery and cook until tender.

2. Stir the broth, black pepper and potatoes in the saucepan and heat to a boil. Reduce the heat to low. Cover and cook for 15 minutes or until the potatoes are tender.

3. Place HALF of the broth mixture and HALF of the milk in a blender or food processor. Cover and blend until smooth. Repeat with the remaining broth mixture and remaining milk. Return to the saucepan and heat through.

PREP TIME: 15 minutes
COOK TIME: 25 minutes
TOTAL TIME: 40 minutes

Creamy Irish Potato Soup

Beer, Caramelized Onion, Bacon and Parmesan Muffins

Makes 12 servings

6 slices bacon, chopped
2 cups chopped onions
3 teaspoons sugar, divided
¼ teaspoon dried thyme
¾ cup Irish lager or regular beer
2 eggs
¼ cup extra virgin olive oil
1½ cups all-purpose flour
¾ cup grated Parmesan cheese
2 teaspoons baking powder
½ teaspoon salt

1. Preheat oven to 375°F. Grease 12 standard (2½-inch) muffin cups.

2. Cook bacon in large skillet over medium heat until crisp, stirring occasionally. Remove bacon to paper towel-lined plate with slotted spoon. Add onions, 1 teaspoon sugar and thyme to skillet; cook 12 minutes or until onion is golden brown, stirring occasionally. Cool 5 minutes; stir in bacon.

3. Whisk lager, eggs and oil in medium bowl. Combine flour, cheese, baking powder, salt and remaining 2 teaspoons sugar in large bowl. Add lager mixture to flour mixture; stir just until moistened. Gently stir in onion mixture. Spoon batter evenly into prepared muffin cups.

4. Bake 15 minutes or until toothpick inserted into centers comes out clean. Cool in pan 5 minutes. Serve warm or at room temperature.

Beer, Caramelized Onion, Bacon and Parmesan Muffins

Split Pea Soup with Ham and Ale
Makes 6 servings

1 tablespoon olive oil
1 cup chopped onion
½ cup chopped carrot
½ cup chopped celery
3 cloves garlic, minced
1 bay leaf
¼ teaspoon dried thyme
1 bottle (12 ounces) Irish ale
4 cups reduced-sodium chicken broth
1 package (16 ounces) green split peas, picked over and rinsed
1 pound smoked ham hocks
2 cups water

1. Heat oil in Dutch oven over medium heat. Add onion, carrot, celery, garlic, bay leaf and thyme; cook 4 to 5 minutes or until vegetables begin to soften, stirring occasionally. Pour in ale; increase heat to medium-high. Bring to a boil; cook 6 to 7 minutes or until reduced by half.

2. Stir in broth, split peas, ham hocks and water. Bring to a boil; reduce heat to medium-low. Cover; simmer about 1 hour or until peas are tender, stirring occasionally.

3. Remove ham hocks; let stand until cool enough to handle. Remove ham from hocks; chop ham and return to Dutch oven. Discard bay leaf.

Split Pea Soup with Ham and Ale

MAIN EVENTS

Baked Cod with Tomatoes and Olives

Makes 4 servings

1 pound cod fillets (about 4 fillets), cut into 2-inch pieces
  Salt and black pepper
1 can (about 14 ounces) diced Italian-style tomatoes, drained
2 tablespoons chopped pitted ripe olives
1 teaspoon minced garlic
2 tablespoons chopped fresh parsley

1. Preheat oven to 400°F. Spray 13×9-inch baking dish with nonstick olive oil cooking spray. Arrange cod fillets in pan; season to taste with salt and pepper.

2. Combine tomatoes, olives and garlic in medium bowl. Spoon over fish.

3. Bake 20 minutes or until fish begins to flake when tested with fork. Sprinkle with parsley.

SERVING SUGGESTION: For a great accompaniment to this dish, spread French bread with softened butter, sprinkle with paprika and oregano, and broil until lightly toasted.

PREP AND COOK TIME: 25 minutes

Beef Wellington
Makes 6 servings

**6 center-cut beef tenderloin steaks, 1 inch thick
(about 2½ pounds)**
¾ teaspoon salt, divided
½ teaspoon black pepper, divided
2 tablespoons butter or margarine
8 ounces cremini or button mushrooms, finely chopped
¼ cup finely chopped shallots
2 tablespoons ruby port or sweet Madeira wine
1 package (about 17 ounces) frozen puff pastry, thawed
1 egg, separated
½ cup (4 ounces) prepared liver pâté*
2 teaspoons water

*Pâté can be found in the gourmet or deli section of most supermarkets or in specialty food stores.

1. Sprinkle steaks with ½ teaspoon salt and ¼ teaspoon pepper. Heat large nonstick skillet over medium-high heat. Cook steaks 3 minutes per side or until well browned. Transfer to plate; let cool.

2. Melt butter in same skillet over medium heat; add mushrooms and shallots. Cook and stir 5 minutes or until mushrooms are tender. Add port, remaining ¼ teaspoon salt and ¼ teaspoon pepper. Bring to a boil. Reduce heat; simmer 10 minutes or until liquid evaporates, stirring often. Cool completely.

3. Roll out each pastry sheet to 18×10-inch rectangle on lightly floured surface. Cut each sheet into 3 (10×6-inch) rectangles. Cut small amount of pastry from corners to use as decoration, if desired.

4. Whisk egg white in small bowl until foamy; brush over pastry. Place one steak on each pastry rectangle. Spread pâté over steaks. Top with mushroom mixture.

5. Fold pastry over steak; press edges to seal. Place seam side down on ungreased baking sheet. Cut pastry scraps into shapes and use to decorate, if desired.

6. Whisk egg yolk and water in small bowl. Brush over pastry; cover loosely with plastic wrap. Refrigerate 1 to 4 hours before baking.

7. Preheat oven to 400°F. Bake 20 to 25 minutes or until pastry is puffed and golden brown and steaks are medium (145°F) or desired doneness. Let stand 10 minutes before serving.

● ◆ ●

Beef Wellington

Mint Marinated Racks of Lamb

Makes 4 servings

2 whole racks (6 ribs each) lamb rib chops (about 3 pounds), well trimmed
1 cup dry red wine
½ cup plus 2 tablespoons chopped fresh mint, divided
3 cloves garlic, minced
¼ cup Dijon mustard
⅔ cup plain dry bread crumbs

1. Place lamb in large resealable food storage bag. Combine wine, ½ cup mint and garlic in small bowl. Pour over lamb chops. Seal bag; turn to coat. Marinate in refrigerator at least 2 hours or up to 4 hours, turning occasionally.

2. Prepare grill for indirect cooking over medium heat.

3. Drain lamb, discarding marinade; pat dry with paper towels. Place lamb in shallow glass dish. Combine mustard and remaining 2 tablespoons mint in small bowl; spread over meaty side of lamb. Pat bread crumbs evenly over mustard mixture.

4. Place lamb, crumb side down, on grid. Grill, covered, 10 minutes. Turn; grill, covered, 20 minutes until 145°F for medium or desired doneness. Transfer lamb to cutting board. Let stand 5 minutes. Slice between ribs into individual chops.

Mint Marinated Racks of Lamb

Roast Dilled Scrod with Asparagus
Makes 4 servings

1 bunch (12 ounces) asparagus spears, ends trimmed
1 tablespoon olive oil
4 scrod or cod fillets (see Tip)
1 tablespoon lemon juice
1 teaspoon dried dill weed
½ teaspoon salt
¼ teaspoon black pepper
Paprika (optional)

1. Preheat oven to 425°F.

2. Place asparagus in 13×9-inch baking dish. Drizzle oil over asparagus. Roll asparagus to coat lightly with oil; push to edges of dish.

3. Arrange fish fillets in dish. Drizzle with lemon juice. Combine dill, salt and pepper in small bowl; sprinkle over fish and asparagus.

4. Roast 15 to 17 minutes or until fish begins to flake when tested with fork and asparagus is crisp-tender.

◆ Tip ◆

Scrod is the name for young cod that weighs less than
2½ pounds. Regular cod, haddock or pollack would also be
delicious in this dish. Don't overcook fish or it can become
dry and tasteless. Remember that it will continue to cook a
bit even after it's removed from the oven.

Roast Dilled Scrod with Asparagus

Salisbury Steaks
with Mushroom-Wine Sauce
Makes 4 servings

1 pound ground beef
¾ teaspoon garlic salt or other seasoned salt
¼ teaspoon black pepper
2 tablespoons butter or margarine
1 package (8 ounces) sliced mushrooms
2 tablespoons sweet vermouth or ruby port wine
1 jar (12 ounces) *or* 1 can (10½ ounces) beef gravy

1. Heat large nonstick skillet over medium-high heat. Combine beef, garlic salt and pepper in medium bowl; mix well. Shape mixture into 4 oval patties.

2. Place patties in skillet; cook 3 minutes per side or until browned. Transfer to plate. Pour off drippings.

3. Melt butter in same skillet; add mushrooms. Cook and stir 2 minutes. Add vermouth; cook 1 minute. Add gravy; mix well.

4. Return patties to skillet; simmer, uncovered, over medium heat 2 minutes or until cooked through (160°F).

PREP AND COOK TIME: 20 minutes

◆ Tip ◆

Serve Salisbury Steak with mashed potatoes or noodles to soak up the sauce and perhaps some peas on the side for color. It may not be steak, but this recipe turns ordinary ground beef into a much fancier meal.

Salisbury Steak with Mushroom-Wine Sauce

Speedy Salmon Patties
Makes 6 patties

1 can (about 14 ounces) salmon, undrained
1 egg, lightly beaten
¼ cup minced green onions
1 tablespoon chopped fresh dill
1 clove garlic, minced
½ cup all-purpose flour
1½ teaspoons baking powder
1½ cups vegetable oil

1. Drain salmon, reserving 2 tablespoons liquid. Place salmon in medium bowl; break apart with fork, removing skin and bones, if desired. Add reserved liquid, egg, green onions, dill and garlic; mix well.

2. Combine flour and baking powder in small bowl; add to salmon mixture. Stir until well blended. Shape mixture into six patties.

3. Heat oil in large skillet to 350°F. Add salmon patties; cook until golden brown on both sides. Remove from oil; drain on paper towels. Serve warm.

 Tip ◆

Canned salmon is a great pantry ingredient to have on hand. It's already cooked and offers essentially the same nutritional benefits as fresh. The bones and skin you'll find in the can are perfectly edible. In fact, the bones are high in calcium and soft enough to break into small pieces. If the look or texture bothers you, remove skin and bones before using the salmon.

Bacon, Onion and Stout Braised Short Ribs

Makes 4 to 6 servings

4 pounds bone-in beef short ribs, well trimmed
1 teaspoon salt, plus additional for seasoning
½ teaspoon ground black pepper, plus additional for seasoning
1 tablespoon vegetable oil
6 ounces thick-cut bacon, chopped
1 large onion, halved and cut into slices
1 tablespoon tomato paste
2 tablespoons all-purpose flour
2 tablespoons spicy brown mustard
1 bottle (12 ounces) Irish stout
1 cup beef broth
1 bay leaf
2 tablespoons finely chopped parsley
   Hot mashed potatoes or cooked egg noodles (optional)

SLOW COOKER DIRECTIONS

1. Season ribs with salt and pepper. Heat oil in large skillet over medium-high heat until almost smoking. Cook ribs in batches, turning to brown all sides. Transfer each batch to slow cooker. Wipe skillet with paper towels.

2. Cook bacon in same skillet over medium heat 4 minutes or until crisp, stirring occasionally. Drain on paper towels. Drain all but 1 tablespoon of drippings from skillet.

3. Add onion to skillet; cook and stir until softened and translucent. Add tomato paste, flour, mustard, 1 teaspoon salt and ½ teaspoon pepper; cook and stir 1 minute. Remove skillet from heat and pour in stout, stirring to scrape up browned bits. Pour over short ribs. Add bacon, broth and bay leaf.

4. Cover; cook on LOW 8 hours.

5. Skim fat from cooking liquid. Remove bay leaf; stir in parsley. Serve with mashed potatoes.

Ham with Dark Beer Gravy
Makes 10 to 12 servings

1 fully cooked bone-in ham (about 6 pounds)
1 tablespoon Dijon mustard
2 cans (6 ounces each) pineapple juice
1 bottle (12 ounces) Irish stout or porter
Dark Beer Gravy (recipe follows)

1. Line large roasting pan with foil.

2. Remove skin and excess fat from ham. Score ham in diamond pattern.

3. Place ham in prepared roasting pan. Spread mustard over ham. Pour pineapple juice and beer over ham. Cover; refrigerate 8 hours.

4. Preheat oven to 350°F. Cook ham 1½ hours or until thermometer inserted into thickest part registers 140°F, basting every 30 minutes. Transfer to cutting board; cover and let stand 15 minutes before slicing.

5. Meanwhile, pour drippings from pan into large measuring cup. Let stand 5 minutes; skim and discard fat. Prepare Dark Beer Gravy.

Dark Beer Gravy
Makes 2½ cups

¼ cup (½ stick) butter
¼ cup all-purpose flour
2 cups drippings from roasting pan
½ cup Irish stout or porter
Salt and black pepper

Melt butter in saucepan over medium heat. Whisk in flour. Cook, whisking constantly, 1 to 2 minutes. Combine drippings and beer in small bowl; whisk into flour mixture. Cook, whisking constantly, until mixture is thickened and bubbly. Season with salt and pepper.

Ham with Dark Beer Gravy

Spiced Pot Roast
Makes 8 servings

3 tablespoons packed brown sugar
2 teaspoons ground cloves
2 teaspoons ground allspice
2 teaspoons ground cinnamon
1 teaspoon cracked black pepper
1 boneless beef bottom round roast or beef chuck pot roast
  (about 4 pounds)
2 cups SWANSON® Beef Stock
1 bottle (12 ounces) dark beer or stout
  Hot boiled potatoes
  Chopped fresh parsley (optional)

1. Stir the brown sugar, cloves, allspice, cinnamon and black pepper in a large bowl. Add the beef and turn to coat. Cover the bowl and refrigerate for 12 hours or overnight.

2. Place the beef in a 6-quart oven-safe saucepot. Pour the stock and beer over the beef. COVER the saucepot.

3. Bake at 350°F. for 3 hours or until the beef is fork-tender. Remove the beef from the saucepot and let stand for 10 minutes. Thinly slice the beef. Serve with the stock mixture and the potatoes. Sprinkle with the parsley, if desired.

PREP TIME: 5 minutes
MARINATE TIME: 12 hours
BAKE TIME: 3 hours
STAND TIME: 10 minutes

Spiced Pot Roast

Braised Lamb Shanks

Makes 4 servings

2 tablespoons all-purpose flour
1 teaspoon salt
½ teaspoon ground black pepper
4 lamb shanks (about 4 to 5 pounds total)
2 to 3 tablespoons olive oil
1 tablespoon butter
1 large onion, chopped
4 cloves garlic, minced
1 cup beef or chicken broth
1 cup dry red wine
**2 tablespoons chopped fresh rosemary leaves *or* 2 teaspoons
    dried rosemary**

1. Preheat oven to 350°F. Combine flour, salt and pepper in large resealable food storage bag. Add lamb shanks, one at a time, to bag; shake to coat lightly. (Use all of flour mixture.)

2. Heat 2 tablespoons oil and butter in large Dutch oven over medium heat. Brown lamb shanks on all sides in batches. Transfer lamb to plate.

3. Add remaining 1 tablespoon oil to Dutch oven, if needed. Add onion and garlic; cook and stir 5 minutes. Stir in broth, wine and rosemary; bring to a boil over high heat.

4. Return lamb and any accumulated juices to Dutch oven. Cover; cook 1½ to 2 hours or until lamb is fork-tender. Transfer lamb to serving platter; keep warm.

5. Skim off and discard fat from juices in Dutch oven. Boil juices until reduced to 2 cups and slightly thickened. (Depending on amount of remaining liquid, this could take from 2 to 10 minutes.) Serve sauce over lamb.

Braised Lamb Shanks

Dill-Crusted Salmon
Makes 4 servings

4 salmon steaks or fillets (about 5 ounces each)
½ cup panko bread crumbs
½ cup fresh dill, finely chopped
3 tablespoons mayonnaise
2 tablespoons olive oil
1 teaspoon salt
½ teaspoon red pepper flakes

1. Preheat oven to 400°F. Spray rack in roasting pan with nonstick cooking spray. Place salmon on rack.

2. Combine bread crumbs, dill, mayonnaise, oil, salt and red pepper flakes in medium bowl; mix well. Divide mixture among salmon, mounding on top; press to adhere.

3. Bake 20 to 25 minutes or until topping is browned and salmon begins to flake when tested with fork.

◆ Tip ◆

Both farmed and wild salmon taste good and are good for you. Salmon flesh varies in color from light pink to deep red. Most wild North American salmon comes from Alaska. King or Chinook salmon weigh up to 120 pounds. Salmon is sold cut into steaks or fillets. Steaks are thick cross sections of the fish, cut perpendicular to the backbone. Fillets are cut parallel to the backbone and are usually tapered toward the tail end.

Dill-Crusted Salmon

Herbed Standing Rib Roast

Makes 16 (6-ounce) servings

2 teaspoons kosher salt
1 (4-rib) bone-in standing rib roast (about 9 pounds)
4 cloves garlic, minced
2 tablespoons chopped fresh rosemary
2 tablespoons chopped fresh thyme
2 tablespoons chopped Italian parsley
2 tablespoons chopped fresh oregano
2 tablespoons olive oil
2 teaspoons grated lemon peel
2 teaspoons black pepper
¼ teaspoon red pepper flakes

1. Sprinkle salt over entire roast. Wrap in plastic wrap and refrigerate at least 2 hours or up to 2 days.

2. Remove roast from refrigerator. Mix garlic, rosemary, thyme, parsley, oregano, oil, lemon peel, black pepper and red pepper flakes into a paste in small bowl. Rub paste all over roast. Allow roast to sit at room temperature at least 1 hour or up to 2 hours.

3. Preheat oven to 450°F. Spray roasting pan with nonstick cooking spray (it should be just large enough to fit the roast). Place roast, bone side down, in prepared pan. Roast 25 minutes. *Reduce oven temperature to 350°F.* Roast an additional 1½ to 2 hours until 140°F for medium-rare or desired doneness. Tent with foil. Let stand 15 to 20 minutes before slicing.

◆ Tip ◆

Garnish roast with sprigs of fresh thyme and/or rosemary.

Herbed Standing Rib Roast

PUB BITES

Pub-Style Fish & Chips
Makes 4 servings

¾ **cup all-purpose flour**
½ **cup flat Irish ale**
   Vegetable oil
3 **large or 4 medium russet potatoes**
1 **egg, separated**
   Salt
1 **pound cod fillets**
   Prepared tartar sauce
   Lemon wedges

1. Combine flour, ale and 2 teaspoons oil in small bowl. Cover; refrigerate 1 to 2 hours.

2. Peel and cut potatoes into thin wedges. Place in large bowl of cold water. Pour at least 2 inches oil into deep, heavy saucepan or deep fryer. Heat over medium heat to 320°F. Drain and thoroughly dry potatoes. Cook in batches about 4 minutes or until slightly softened but not browned. Drain on paper towels. Reserve oil to fry cod.

3. Stir egg yolk into reserved flour mixture. Beat egg white in medium bowl with electric mixer at medium-high speed until soft peaks form. Fold egg white into flour mixture. Season batter with pinch of salt.

4. Heat oil to 360°F. Cut fish into long pieces 2 to 3 inches wide. Remove any pin bones. Dip into batter, shaking off excess. Lower carefully into oil and cook 4 to 6 minutes or until batter is browned and fish is cooked through, turning once. Cook fish in batches and do not crowd pan. (Allow temperature of oil to return to 360°F between batches.) Drain on paper towels and keep warm.

5. Return potato wedges to hot oil; cook in batches 5 minutes or until browned and crisp. Drain and sprinkle with salt. Serve with tartar sauce and lemon wedges.

Bacon and Cheese Rarebit
Makes 6 servings

1½ tablespoons butter
½ cup Irish lager
2 teaspoons Worcestershire sauce
2 teaspoons Dijon mustard
⅛ teaspoon ground red pepper
2 cups (8 ounces) shredded American cheese
1½ cups (6 ounces) shredded sharp Cheddar cheese
1 small loaf (8 ounces) egg bread or challah, cut into
    6 (1-inch-thick) slices
12 large slices tomato
12 slices bacon, crisp-cooked

1. Preheat broiler.

2. Melt butter in double boiler set over simmering water. Stir in beer, Worcestershire sauce, mustard and red pepper. Cook until heated through, stirring occasionally. Gradually add cheeses, stirring constantly until melted. Remove from heat; cover and keep warm.

3. Broil bread slices until golden brown. Arrange on greased or foil-lined baking sheet. Top each serving with tomato slices and bacon slices. Spoon about ¼ cup cheese sauce evenly over top. Broil 4 to 5 inches from heat just until cheese sauce begins to brown. Serve immediately.

Bacon and Cheese Rarebit

Mussels in Beer Broth
Makes 4 servings

2 tablespoons olive oil
⅓ cup chopped shallots
4 cloves garlic, minced
2 cups Irish ale
1 can (about 14 ounces) Italian-style diced tomatoes
¼ cup chopped fresh parsley
1 tablespoon chopped fresh thyme
½ teaspoon salt
¼ teaspoon red pepper flakes
3 pounds mussels, scrubbed and debearded
French bread (optional)

1. Heat oil in large saucepan or Dutch oven. Add shallots and garlic; cook and stir 3 minutes or until tender. Stir in ale, tomatoes, parsley, thyme, salt and red pepper flakes. Bring to a boil over medium-high heat.

2. Add mussels. Reduce heat to low; cover and simmer 5 to 7 minutes or until mussels open. Discard any unopened mussels. Serve with French bread, if desired.

◆ Tip ◆

To prepare mussels for cooking, scrub them with a brush under cold water. Don't leave them soaking as it may kill them. Throw away any mussels with cracked or broken shells. If any mussels have open shells, tap them sharply on a hard surface to see if they close. If they don't, discard them since that means they are no longer alive. Remove the beard by pulling it firmly from the tip of the mussel toward the hinge.

Mussels in Beer Broth

Reuben Rolls
Makes 8 rolls

1 cup sauerkraut
1 container (about 14 ounces) refrigerated pizza dough
6 thin slices Swiss cheese (about 4 ounces)
1 teaspoon caraway seeds
½ teaspoon black pepper
⅓ pound thinly sliced corned beef
Prepared Thousand Island dressing

1. Preheat oven to 400°F. Line baking sheet with parchment paper. Squeeze sauerkraut as dry as possible to yield about ⅔ cup.

2. Unroll dough on clean work surface; press into 13×9-inch rectangle. Arrange cheese slices evenly over dough, leaving 1 inch border on all sides. Top with sauerkraut; sprinkle with caraway seeds and pepper. Top with corned beef slices.

3. Starting from long side, gently roll up dough and filling jelly-roll style. Trim off ends. Cut into 8 (1½ inch) slices with serrated knife. Place slices cut side up on prepared baking sheet.

4. Bake 20 to 25 minutes or until golden brown and cheese is melted. Immediately remove from baking sheet; serve warm with dressing for dipping.

Reuben Rolls

Roasted Garlic & Stout Mac & Cheese

Makes 8 to 10 servings

1 head garlic
1 tablespoon olive oil
6 tablespoons unsalted butter, divided
1¼ teaspoons salt, divided
1 cup panko bread crumbs
¼ cup all-purpose flour
½ teaspoon black pepper
2 cups whole milk
¾ cup Irish stout
2 cups (8 ounces) shredded sharp Cheddar cheese
2 cups (8 ounces) shredded Dubliner cheese
1 pound cellentani pasta*, cooked and drained

*Substitute elbow macaroni, penne or other favorite pasta shape.

1. Preheat oven to 375°F. Butter shallow 4-quart baking dish.

2. Place garlic on 10-inch piece of foil, drizzle with olive oil and crimp shut. Place on small baking sheet and bake 30 minutes or until tender. Unwrap, cool 15 minutes, then squeeze cloves out into a small bowl. Mash into smooth paste.

3. Microwave 2 tablespoons of butter in medium microwavable bowl until melted. Stir in ¼ teaspoon salt until dissolved. Toss bread crumbs with melted butter until evenly coated; set aside.

4. Melt remaining 4 tablespoons butter in large saucepan over medium heat. Add flour; cook and stir until light brown. Stir in roasted garlic paste, remaining 1 teaspoon salt and black pepper. Slowly whisk in milk and stout. Simmer until thickened, whisking constantly. Remove from heat; whisk in shredded cheeses, ½ cup at a time, until melted.

5. Combine cheese mixture and pasta in large bowl. Transfer to prepared baking dish; sprinkle evenly with bread crumbs. Bake 40 minutes or until bubbly and topping is golden brown. Let stand 10 minutes before serving.

Roasted Garlic & Stout Mac & Cheese

Spicy Ale Shrimp
Makes 15 to 20 shrimp

3 bottles (12 ounces each) Irish ale, divided
1 tablespoon seafood boil seasoning blend
1 teaspoon mustard seeds
1 teaspoon red pepper flakes
1 lemon, cut into wedges, divided
1 pound large raw shrimp, peeled and deveined (with tails on)
   Dipping Sauce (recipe follows) and additional lemon wedges

1. Prepare Dipping Sauce.

2. Fill large saucepan half full with water. Add 2 bottles of ale, seasoning blend, mustard seeds and red pepper flakes. Squeeze lemon juice into saucepan and add lemon wedges. Bring mixture to a boil over medium-high heat.

3. Meanwhile, pour remaining bottle of ale into large bowl half full of ice; set aside.

4. Add shrimp to saucepan. Cover; remove from heat. Let stand 3 minutes or until shrimp are pink and opaque. Drain; transfer shrimp to bowl of chilled ale and ice. Cool. Remove shrimp from bowl; arrange on platter. Serve with Dipping Sauce and additional lemon wedges.

Dipping Sauce
Makes about 1 cup sauce

1 cup ketchup
1 tablespoon prepared horseradish
1 to 2 teaspoons chili-garlic paste
   Juice of one lime

Combine ketchup, horseradish, chili-garlic paste and lime juice in small bowl. Cover; refrigerate 1 hour.

Lamb-Sicles

Makes 4 servings

6 cloves garlic
1 teaspoon salt
2 tablespoons finely chopped fresh rosemary leaves
2 tablespoons olive oil
2 teaspoons Dijon mustard
½ teaspoon ground black pepper
12 small lamb rib chops, bone-in and frenched*
Mint jelly

*The term frenched means that the fat and meat have been cut away from the end of the bone protruding from the chop. Ask the butcher to do this for you if frenched chops are not available already cut. You can also purchase a frenched rack of lamb and cut it into individual chops.

1. Chop garlic with salt until finely minced. Place in small bowl; add rosemary, oil and pepper. Mix well.

2. Rub mixture on both sides of chops; wrap in single layer in foil and refrigerate 30 minutes to 3 hours.

3. Prepare grill for direct cooking. Grill chops on well-oiled grid over medium-high heat 2 to 5 minutes per side or until 145°F for medium-rare or desired doneness. Lamb should feel slightly firm when pressed. (To check doneness, cut small slit in meat near bone; lamb should be rosy pink.)

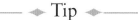 Tip ◆

Grilling lamb chops is quick, easy and delicious, but it's important to start with the right kind of chops. Loin, rib or sirloin chops are tender enough for quick cooking. Shoulder or leg chops need longer, moister cooking methods to make them tender. To be called lamb, the sheep must be less than one year old. Mutton comes from animals over 2 years old and is tougher and stronger in flavor.

Potted Beer and Cheddar

Makes about 3 cups

8 ounces cream cheese, softened
4 tablespoons CABOT® Unsalted Butter, softened
4 cups grated CABOT® Sharp Cheddar (about 1 pound)
1 tablespoon minced fresh chives
1 tablespoon chopped fresh parsley
1 teaspoon Worcestershire sauce
1 teaspoon Dijon mustard
1 teaspoon prepared horseradish
½ clove garlic, minced
¼ teaspoon ground black pepper
2 to 3 drops hot pepper sauce
¼ to ½ cup flat beer

1. With electric mixer, beat together cream cheese and butter until well blended. Mix in cheese.

2. Mix in all remaining ingredients except beer. Add enough beer to make spread of desired consistency (mixture will thicken further after chilling).

3. Pack into earthenware crock or other ceramic dish; cover and refrigerate for several hours to allow flavors to blend. Serve with apple slices and dark rye bread or crackers.

NOTE: Spread can be made several weeks in advance.

Potted Beer and Cheddar

Mini Smoked Salmon Latkes

Makes about 24 appetizers

**2 cups frozen shredded hash brown potatoes, thawed and
    drained**
1 egg, lightly beaten
2 tablespoons finely chopped shallot
1 tablespoon all-purpose flour
1 tablespoon whipping cream
½ teaspoon salt
¼ teaspoon black pepper
1 tablespoon butter, divided
1 tablespoon vegetable oil, divided
1 package (4 ounces) smoked salmon, cut into 24 pieces
Sour cream
Whitefish or lumpfish caviar (optional)*

**Red or black lumpfish caviar is available in jars at the supermarket. It's usually stocked near the
tuna and other canned fish. It's an affordable way to capture the mystique of caviar.*

1. Chop potatoes into smaller pieces. Combine potatoes, egg, shallot, flour, cream, salt and pepper in large bowl; mix well.

2. Heat 1½ teaspoons butter and 1½ teaspoons oil in large nonstick skillet over medium-high heat. Spoon tablespoonfuls of potato mixture into skillet; flatten with spatula to make small pancakes. Cook 3 minutes on each side. Remove to plate. Repeat with remaining butter, oil and potato mixture.

3. Top each pancake with small piece of smoked salmon, dollop of sour cream and pinch of caviar, if desired. Serve immediately.

Mini Smoked Salmon Latkes

Beer-Battered Mushrooms

Makes 6 to 8 servings

Vegetable oil
1 cup all-purpose flour
½ teaspoon baking powder
½ teaspoon chili powder
¼ teaspoon salt, plus extra for seasoning
⅛ teaspoon black pepper
1 cup beer
1 egg, separated
1 pound mushrooms

1. Heat 1½ to 2½ inches oil in large saucepan or deep fryer to 365°F. Mix flour, baking powder, chili powder, salt and black pepper in medium bowl. Whisk beer and egg yolk in small bowl.

2. Beat egg white in medium bowl with electric mixer at medium speed until soft peaks form.

3. Stir beer mixture into flour mixture just until blended. Fold in egg white.

4. Dip mushrooms into batter in batches and carefully place in hot oil. Fry mushrooms 2 minutes or until golden brown, turning occasionally. (Stir batter and allow oil to return to temperature between batches.) Remove mushrooms to paper towels to drain; immediately season with salt.

Beer-Battered Mushrooms

Leek Cheese Pie

Makes 6 servings

⅔ cup thinly sliced leek
¼ cup water
1 clove garlic, minced
1 cup all-purpose flour
2 teaspoons baking powder
4 egg whites, divided
¼ cup milk
1½ tablespoons canola oil
¼ cup cream cheese, softened
1 carton (12 ounces) dry curd cottage cheese or farmer cheese
¾ cup shredded carrot
2 tablespoons fine dry bread crumbs
2 tablespoons chopped fresh basil *or* 2 teaspoons dried basil
¼ teaspoon black pepper

1. Preheat oven to 325°F. Coat 9-inch pie plate with nonstick cooking spray. Combine leek, water and garlic in small saucepan. Bring to a boil over high heat. Reduce heat to medium-low. Cover; simmer 3 to 4 minutes or until leek is tender. Drain.

2. Combine flour and baking powder in medium bowl. Stir in leek mixture, 2 egg whites, milk and oil until nearly smooth. Spread half of batter into prepared pie plate. Bake 20 to 22 minutes or until crust is beginning to brown.

3. Meanwhile, combine remaining 2 egg whites and cream cheese in medium bowl. Stir in cottage cheese, carrot, bread crumbs, basil and pepper. Spread over crust. Spoon remaining batter on top. Bake 40 to 45 minutes or until golden brown. Let stand 10 minutes before serving.

Leek Cheese Pie

Mini Cheddar-Beer Biscuits with Ham

Makes 12 servings

2 cups all-purpose flour
1 tablespoon baking powder
½ teaspoon salt
1 cup (about 4 ounces) shredded Cheddar cheese
¼ cup shortening
¾ cup Irish lager
1 egg, lightly beaten
8 slices cooked deli ham
1 tablespoon honey mustard

1. Preheat oven to 425°F. Grease baking sheets. Combine flour, baking powder and salt in large bowl. Stir in cheese. Cut in shortening with pastry blender or two knives until mixture resembles coarse crumbs. Add lager; stir just until combined.

2. Divide dough in half. Pat half of dough on prepared baking sheet into 6×4½-inch rectangle, about ½ inch thick. Score dough into 12 squares. Repeat with remaining dough. Brush tops with egg.

3. Bake 17 minutes or until golden brown. Cool on baking sheet 2 minutes. Remove to wire racks; cool completely.

4. Cut each rectangle in half horizontally. Arrange slices of ham to cover bottoms. Spread mustard on biscuit tops; place on ham. Cut into 24 individual biscuits along score lines.

Mini Cheddar-Beer Biscuits with Ham

DUBLINER DESSERTS

White Chocolate Shamrocks
Makes about 2 dozen cookies

**2 packages (about 16 ounces each) refrigerated sugar
  cookie dough**
½ cup all-purpose flour
  Green food coloring
1 package (14 ounces) white chocolate candy discs
  Green and white sprinkles, dragées or decorating sugar

1. Let doughs stand at room temperature 15 minutes. Lightly grease cookie sheets.

2. Preheat oven to 350°F. Beat doughs, flour and food coloring, a few drops at a time, in large bowl with electric mixer at medium speed until well blended. Reserve half of dough; wrap and refrigerate.

3. Roll out remaining dough between sheets of parchment paper to ¼-inch thickness. Cut out shapes using 2-inch shamrock cookie cutter. Place 2 inches apart on prepared cookie sheets. Repeat with reserved dough. Refrigerate 15 minutes.

4. Bake 8 to 10 minutes or until set. Cool on cookie sheets 5 minutes. Remove to wire racks; cool completely.

5. Microwave candy discs in medium microwavable bowl on HIGH 1 minute. Stir. Microwave at additional 15-second intervals until smooth and spreadable. Dip edge of each cookie into melted chocolate; decorate with sprinkles. Let stand on parchment paper 15 minutes or until set.

Chocolate Stout Cake
Makes 12 servings

2 cups all-purpose flour
¾ cup unsweetened cocoa
1 teaspoon baking soda
¼ teaspoon salt
¾ cup (1½ sticks) butter, softened
1 cup packed light brown sugar
½ cup granulated sugar
1 teaspoon vanilla
3 eggs
1 cup Irish stout, at room temperature
Cream Cheese Frosting (recipe follows)

1. Preheat oven to 350°F. Spray 13×9-inch baking pan with nonstick cooking spray. Combine flour, cocoa, baking soda and salt in medium bowl; set aside.

2. Beat butter, brown sugar and granulated sugar with electric mixer at medium speed until light and fluffy. Beat in vanilla. Add eggs, one at a time, beating after each addition. Add flour mixture alternately with stout, beating after each addition. Pour batter evenly into prepared pan.

3. Bake 35 to 40 minutes or until toothpick inserted into center comes out clean. Cool on wire rack.

4. Prepare Cream Cheese Frosting. Spread frosting over cake.

Cream Cheese Frosting

1 (8-ounce) package cream cheese, softened
¼ cup (½ stick) butter, softened
4 cups powdered sugar
1 teaspoon vanilla
1 to 2 tablespoons milk

Beat cream cheese and butter with electric mixer at medium speed until creamy. Gradually beat in powdered sugar and vanilla until smooth. Add enough milk to make frosting easy to spread.

Chocolate Stout Cake

Leprechaun Cupcakes
Makes 24 cupcakes

**1 package (about 18 ounces) yellow or white cake mix, plus
    ingredients to prepare mix**
Chocolate wafer cookies
1 container (16 ounces) white frosting
Green food coloring
Yellow chewy fruit candy squares
Black licorice ropes and strings
Black decorating gel
Red gumdrops
White decors
Orange decorating icing

1. Preheat oven to 350°F. Line 24 standard (2½-inch) muffin cups with paper baking cups. Prepare cake mix according to package directions. Spoon batter into prepared muffin cups, filling two-thirds full.

2. Bake 20 minutes or until toothpick inserted into centers comes out clean. Cool in pans 10 minutes. Remove to wire racks; cool completely.

3. Trim chocolate wafer cookies into trapezoid shapes for hats as shown in photo. Place ½ cup frosting in small bowl. Add food coloring, a few drops at a time, until desired shade of green is reached. Spread green frosting over wafer cookies. Frost cupcakes with remaining white frosting.

4. Working with one at a time, unwrap chewy candy squares and microwave on LOW (30%) 5 seconds or until slightly softened. Press candy between hands or on waxed paper to flatten slightly; trim into square shapes for hat buckles. Trim licorice ropes into 2- to 3-inch lengths for hat brims. Press frosted wafers onto one edge of cupcakes. Adhere brims and buckles using dots of gel.

5. Roll out red gumdrops on generously sugared surface. Cut out small pieces to resemble mouths; place on cupcakes. Place decors on cupcakes for eyes; pipe dot of gel in center of each. Trim licorice strings and place on cupcakes for eyebrows. Pipe orange decorating icing around edges of cupcakes for beards and sideburns.

Leprechaun Cupcakes

Apple-Buttermilk Pie
Makes 8 servings

2 medium Granny Smith or other baking apples
1 (9-inch) unbaked pie shell
3 eggs
1½ cups sugar, divided
1 cup buttermilk
⅓ cup butter, melted
2 tablespoons all-purpose flour
2 teaspoons ground cinnamon, divided
2 teaspoons vanilla
¾ teaspoon ground nutmeg, divided

1. Preheat oven to 350°F. Peel and core apples; cut into small chunks. Place in pie shell.

2. Beat eggs in medium bowl with electric mixer at low speed until blended. Add all but 1 teaspoon sugar, buttermilk, butter, flour, 1 teaspoon cinnamon, vanilla and ½ teaspoon nutmeg; mix at low speed until well blended. Pour buttermilk mixture over apples.

3. Combine remaining 1 teaspoon sugar, 1 teaspoon cinnamon and ¼ teaspoon nutmeg; sprinkle over top.

4. Bake 50 to 60 minutes. Serve warm or at room temperature. Store in refrigerator.

◆ Tip ◆

There are many varieties of apples available in stores and farmers' markets these days. For pies, pick apples with a good tart-sweet flavor when fresh and those that hold their shape without becoming mushy after cooking. Granny Smith has always been a favorite, but Jonathon, Cortland and Braeburn apples are also good choices.

Apple-Buttermilk Pie

Irish Soda Bread Cookies
Makes about 3 dozen cookies

2 cups all-purpose flour
½ teaspoon baking soda
¼ teaspoon salt
½ cup (1 stick) butter, softened
½ cup sugar
1 egg
¾ cup currants
1 teaspoon caraway seeds
⅓ cup buttermilk

1. Preheat oven to 350°F. Line cookie sheets with parchment paper.

2. Combine flour, baking soda and salt in medium bowl.

3. Beat butter and sugar in large bowl with electric mixer at medium speed until fluffy. Add egg; beat 1 minute or until combined. Add flour mixture; beat on low speed until combined. Add currants and caraway seeds; mix well. Add buttermilk; mix until combined.

4. Drop tablespoonfuls of dough 1 inch apart on prepared cookie sheets. Bake 12 to 15 minutes or until light brown. Remove to wire racks; serve warm.

Mint Chocolate Chip Milk Shakes
Makes 2 servings

2 cups mint chocolate chip ice cream
1 cup milk
2 tablespoons whipped topping
1 tablespoon mini chocolate chips

1. Combine ice cream and milk in blender; process until smooth.

2. Pour into two glasses. Top with whipped topping; sprinkle with chocolate chips.

Irish Soda Bread Cookies

Fireside Steamed Pudding
Makes 12 to 14 servings

1½ cups plain dry bread crumbs
1 cup sugar, divided
2 tablespoons all-purpose flour
½ teaspoon baking powder
⅛ teaspoon salt
6 eggs, separated
1 can (21 ounces) cherry pie filling, divided
2 tablespoons butter or margarine, melted
½ teaspoon almond extract
¼ teaspoon red food color
1 cup HERSHEY₅S Mini Chips Semi-Sweet Chocolate
  Cherry Whipped Cream (recipe follows)

1. Thoroughly grease 8-cup tube mold or heat-proof bowl.

2. Stir together bread crumbs, ¾ cup sugar, flour, baking powder and salt in large bowl. Stir together egg yolks, 1½ cups cherry pie filling, butter, almond extract and food color in medium bowl; add to crumb mixture, stirring gently until well blended.

3. Beat egg whites in another large bowl until foamy; gradually add remaining ¼ cup sugar, beating until stiff peaks form. Fold about one-third beaten whites into cherry mixture, blending thoroughly. Fold in remaining egg whites; gently fold in chocolate chips. Pour batter into prepared tube mold. (If mold is open at top, cover opening with foil; grease top of foil.) Cover mold with wax paper and foil; tie securely with string.

4. Place rack in large kettle; pour water into kettle to top of rack. Heat water to boiling; place mold on rack. Cover kettle; steam over simmering water about 1½ hours or until wooden pick inserted comes out clean. (Additional water may be needed during steaming.) Remove from heat; cool in pan 5 minutes. Remove cover; unmold onto serving plate. Serve warm with Cherry Whipped Cream.

CHERRY WHIPPED CREAM: Beat 1 cup (½ pint) cold whipping cream with ¼ cup powdered sugar in medium bowl until stiff; fold in pie filling remaining from pudding (about ½ cup) and ½ teaspoon almond extract.

Fireside Steamed Pudding

Molded Irish Shortbread
Makes 1 shortbread mold

1½ cups all-purpose flour
¼ teaspoon salt
¾ cup butter, softened
⅓ cup sugar
1 egg

1. Preheat oven to temperature recommended by shortbread mold manufacturer. Spray 10-inch ceramic shortbread mold with nonstick cooking spray.

2. Combine flour and salt in medium bowl. Beat butter and sugar in large bowl with electric mixer at medium speed until light and fluffy. Add egg; beat until well blended. Gradually add flour mixture. Beat at low speed until well blended.

3. Press dough firmly into mold. Bake, cool and remove from mold according to manufacturer's directions.

NOTE: If shortbread mold is not available, preheat oven to 350°F. Shape dough into 1-inch balls. Place 2 inches apart on ungreased cookie sheets; press with fork to flatten. Bake 18 to 20 minutes or until edges are lightly browned. Let cookies stand on cookie sheets 2 minutes; transfer to wire racks to cool completely. Makes 2 dozen cookies.

◆ Tip ◆

Butter can be stored in the refrigerator up to 1 month.
Be sure to wrap it airtight, as butter readily absorbs flavors
and odors from other items in the refrigerator.

Irish Whiskey Cake
Makes 16 servings

1 cup cooked, puréed NC sweet potato
½ cup butter
¾ cup granulated sugar
½ cup light brown sugar
½ cup dark brown sugar
4 eggs, room temperature
3 cups flour
1 teaspoon baking powder
1 teaspoon salt
½ cup milk
Irish Whiskey Glaze (recipe follows)

1. Preheat oven to 325°F. Grease and flour a standard tube pan.

2. Cream butter with sugars in a large mixing bowl. Mix in sweet potato purée. Add eggs, one at a time, beating well after each addition.

3. Sift flour, baking powder and salt together and add alternately with milk to sweet potato mixture. Pour into pan and bake 60 to 70 minutes or until an inserted toothpick comes out clean. Meanwhile, prepare Irish Whiskey Glaze.

Favorite recipe from NORTH CAROLINA SWEETPOTATO COMMISSION

Irish Whiskey Glaze
Makes about 1 cup

1 cup Irish whiskey
2 tablespoons brown sugar
2 tablespoons confectioner's sugar
1 tablespoon butter

1. Combine whiskey, sugars and butter in small saucepan. Slowly heat until sugar is dissolved.

2. Pour a portion of glaze over hot cake in pan. Let soak in a little before adding all glaze. Cool in pan and gently remove to plate.

Favorite recipe from NORTH CAROLINA SWEETPOTATO COMMISSION

Gingerbread with Lemon Sauce
Makes 9 servings

2½ cups all-purpose flour
1½ teaspoons ground cinnamon
1 teaspoon ground ginger
½ teaspoon baking soda
½ teaspoon salt
¾ cup packed light brown sugar
½ cup (1 stick) butter, softened
⅓ cup light molasses
1 egg
¾ cup Irish stout, at room temperature
Lemon Sauce (recipe follows)
Grated lemon peel (optional)

1. Preheat oven to 350°F. Spray bottom of 9-inch square baking pan with nonstick cooking spray. Combine flour, cinnamon, ginger, baking soda and salt in medium bowl; set aside.

2. Beat brown sugar and butter with electric mixer on medium speed until light and fluffy. Add molasses and egg; beat well. Add flour mixture alternately with stout, beating after each addition. Pour batter evenly into prepared pan.

3. Bake 35 to 40 minutes or until toothpick inserted into center comes out clean. Cool on wire rack. Cut into 9 squares.

4. Prepare Lemon Sauce. Top each gingerbread square with Lemon Sauce and sprinkle with grated lemon peel.

Lemon Sauce

1 cup granulated sugar
¾ cup whipping cream
½ cup (1 stick) butter
1 tablespoon lemon juice
2 teaspoons grated lemon peel

Combine granulated sugar, cream and butter in small saucepan. Cook and stir over medium heat until butter is melted. Reduce heat to low; simmer 5 minutes. Stir in lemon juice and peel. Cool slightly.

● ◆ ●

Gingerbread with Lemon Sauce

Individual Irish Coffee Baked Alaska

Makes 4 servings

2 cups vanilla ice cream, softened
2 cups coffee ice cream, softened

CAKE

⅔ cup sugar
3 eggs, separated
⅓ cup all-purpose flour
⅓ cup unsweetened cocoa powder
¼ cup cornstarch
2 tablespoons Irish cream liqueur

MERINGUE

4 egg whites
½ cup sugar
3 tablespoons Irish whiskey

1. Preheat oven to 350°F. Line 4 (1-cup) ramekins with plastic wrap. Place ½ cup vanilla ice cream in each ramekin. Top with ½ cup coffee ice cream. Fold plastic down on top of ice cream. Freeze 4 hours or until firm.

FOR CAKE

2. Line 13×9-inch baking pan with waxed paper. Beat sugar and egg yolks in medium bowl with electric mixer at high speed 4 minutes or until pale and thick; set aside. Beat egg whites in clean medium bowl at high speed until stiff peaks form. Sift flour, cocoa and cornstarch into yolk mixture; stir gently until blended. Fold in egg whites. Carefully spread mixture into prepared baking pan. Bake 10 minutes or until cake springs back lightly when touched. Cool completely in pan on wire rack. Cut cake into 3-inch rounds with cookie or biscuit cutter. Place rounds on top of ice cream in ramekins. Brush rounds with liqueur. Freeze until ready to top with meringue.

FOR MERINGUE

3. Preheat oven to 525°F. Beat egg whites in clean medium bowl at high speed until foamy. Slowly add sugar, beating until stiff, glossy peaks form.

4. Remove desserts from ramekins using plastic wrap. Discard plastic wrap. Place desserts, cake side down, on baking sheet. Spread ⅔ cup meringue over each dessert, working quickly to prevent ice cream from melting. Bake 2 minutes or until meringue is golden.

5. Heat whiskey in small skillet over low heat 1 minute. *Do not boil.* Using long-handled match, ignite whiskey. Carefully pour over each dessert. Allow whiskey to burn out; serve immediately.

Individual Irish Coffee Baked Alaska

Strawberry Rhubarb Pie

Makes 8 servings

Double-Crust Pie Pastry (recipe follows)
1½ cups sugar
½ cup cornstarch
2 tablespoons quick-cooking tapioca
1 tablespoon grated lemon peel
¼ teaspoon ground allspice
4 cups sliced rhubarb
3 cups sliced strawberries
1 egg, lightly beaten

1. Prepare Double-Crust Pie Pastry.

2. Preheat oven to 425°F. Roll out one disc of dough into 11-inch circle on floured surface. Line 9-inch pie plate with pastry.

3. Combine sugar, cornstarch, tapioca, lemon peel and allspice in large bowl. Add rhubarb and strawberries; toss to coat. Transfer to crust. (Do not mound in center.)

4. Roll out remaining pastry into 10-inch circle. Cut into ½-inch-wide strips. Arrange in lattice design over fruit. Seal and flute edge. Brush pastry with egg.

5. Bake 50 minutes or until pastry is golden brown and filling is thick and bubbly. Cool on wire rack. Serve warm or at room temperature.

DOUBLE-CRUST PIE PASTRY: Combine 2½ cups all-purpose flour, 1 teaspoon salt and 1 teaspoon sugar in large bowl. Cut in 1 cup (2 sticks) cubed unsalted butter with pastry blender or two knives until mixture resembles coarse crumbs. Drizzle ⅓ cup water over flour mixture, 2 tablespoons at a time, stirring just until dough comes together. Divide dough in half. Shape each half into disc; wrap in plastic wrap. Refrigerate 30 minutes.

Strawberry Rhubarb Pie

Peach-Ginger Crumble
Makes 6 servings

1 pound frozen sliced peaches, thawed
2 ripe pears, sliced
¾ cup dried apricots, cut into ¼-inch pieces
4 tablespoons packed dark brown sugar, divided
1 tablespoon cornstarch
1 teaspoon vanilla
12 gingersnaps
1 tablespoon canola oil
½ teaspoon ground cinnamon
    Whipped cream (optional)

1. Preheat oven to 350°F. Lightly coat 9-inch deep-dish pie plate with nonstick cooking spray.

2. Combine peaches, pears, apricots, 2 tablespoons brown sugar, cornstarch and vanilla in large bowl; toss until well blended. Transfer to prepared pie plate.

3. Place gingersnaps in large resealable food storage bag. Crush cookies with rolling pin to form coarse crumbs. Combine crumbs, remaining 2 tablespoons brown sugar, oil and cinnamon; mix well. Sprinkle evenly over peach mixture.

4. Bake 30 minutes or until fruit is hot and bubbly. Cool 10 minutes in pan on wire rack. Top with whipped cream.

Irish Coffee
Makes 1 serving

6 ounces freshly brewed strong black coffee
2 teaspoons brown sugar
2 ounces Irish whiskey
¼ cup whipping cream

Combine coffee and brown sugar in Irish coffee glass or mug. Stir in whiskey. Pour cream over back of spoon into coffee.

Peach-Ginger Crumble

Irish Flag Cookies
Makes 2 dozen cookies

1½ cups all-purpose flour
1 teaspoon baking powder
½ teaspoon salt
¾ cup granulated sugar
¾ cup packed light brown sugar
½ cup (1 stick) butter, softened
2 eggs
2 teaspoons vanilla
1 package (12 ounces) semisweet chocolate chips
Prepared white frosting
Green and orange food coloring and decorating gels

1. Preheat oven to 350°F. Grease 13×9-inch baking pan. Combine flour, baking powder and salt in small bowl.

2. Beat granulated sugar, brown sugar and butter in large bowl with electric mixer at medium speed until light and fluffy. Beat in eggs and vanilla. Add flour mixture; beat at low speed until well blended. Stir in chocolate chips. Spread batter evenly in prepared pan. Bake 25 to 30 minutes or until golden brown. Cool completely in pan on wire rack. Cut into 3¼×1½-inch bars.

3. Divide frosting among three small bowls. Tint one with green food coloring and one with orange food coloring. Leave remaining frosting white. Frost individual cookies as shown in photo.

Irish Flag Cookies

Chocolate Shamrock Bread Pudding
Makes 12 servings

10 slices bread, cubed (6 cups)
2 cans (12 ounces each) NESTLÉ® CARNATION® Evaporated Lowfat 2% Milk
2 cups (12-ounce package) NESTLÉ® TOLL HOUSE® Semi-Sweet Chocolate Morsels, *divided*
8 large egg yolks, beaten
¾ cup granulated sugar
½ cup Irish cream liqueur
¼ teaspoon salt
Whipped cream (optional)
NESTLÉ® TOLL HOUSE® Baking Cocoa (optional)

PREHEAT oven to 350°F. Grease 13×9-inch baking dish. Place bread cubes in prepared baking dish.

HEAT evaporated milk in medium saucepan over MEDIUM-HIGH heat; bring just to a boil. Remove from heat. Add *1½ cups* morsels; whisk until smooth.

COMBINE egg yolks, sugar, liqueur and salt in large bowl. Slowly add milk mixture; whisk until smooth. Pour over bread; pressing bread into milk mixture.

BAKE for 35 to 40 minutes or until knife inserted in center comes out clean. Top with *remaining ½ cup* morsels. Serve warm with a dollop of whipped cream and dusting of cocoa.

PREP TIME: 20 minutes
COOKING TIME: 40 minutes

Acknowledgments

The publisher would like to thank the companies and organizations listed below for the use of their recipes and photographs in this publication.

American Lamb Board

Bob Evans®

Cabot® Creamery Cooperative

Campbell Soup Company

Cream of Wheat® Cereal

Crystal Farms®

The Hershey Company

Nestlé USA

North Carolina SweetPotato Commission

The Quaker® Oatmeal Kitchens

Sargento® Foods Inc.

METRIC CONVERSION CHART

VOLUME MEASUREMENTS (dry)

1/8 teaspoon = 0.5 mL
1/4 teaspoon = 1 mL
1/2 teaspoon = 2 mL
3/4 teaspoon = 4 mL
1 teaspoon = 5 mL
1 tablespoon = 15 mL
2 tablespoons = 30 mL
1/4 cup = 60 mL
1/3 cup = 75 mL
1/2 cup = 125 mL
2/3 cup = 150 mL
3/4 cup = 175 mL
1 cup = 250 mL
2 cups = 1 pint = 500 mL
3 cups = 750 mL
4 cups = 1 quart = 1 L

VOLUME MEASUREMENTS (fluid)

1 fluid ounce (2 tablespoons) = 30 mL
4 fluid ounces (1/2 cup) = 125 mL
8 fluid ounces (1 cup) = 250 mL
12 fluid ounces (1 1/2 cups) = 375 mL
16 fluid ounces (2 cups) = 500 mL

WEIGHTS (mass)

1/2 ounce = 15 g
1 ounce = 30 g
3 ounces = 90 g
4 ounces = 120 g
8 ounces = 225 g
10 ounces = 285 g
12 ounces = 360 g
16 ounces = 1 pound = 450 g

DIMENSIONS

1/16 inch = 2 mm
1/8 inch = 3 mm
1/4 inch = 6 mm
1/2 inch = 1.5 cm
3/4 inch = 2 cm
1 inch = 2.5 cm

OVEN TEMPERATURES

250°F = 120°C
275°F = 140°C
300°F = 150°C
325°F = 160°C
350°F = 180°C
375°F = 190°C
400°F = 200°C
425°F = 220°C
450°F = 230°C

BAKING PAN SIZES

Utensil	Size in Inches/Quarts	Metric Volume	Size in Centimeters
Baking or Cake Pan (square or rectangular)	8×8×2	2 L	20×20×5
	9×9×2	2.5 L	23×23×5
	12×8×2	3 L	30×20×5
	13×9×2	3.5 L	33×23×5
Loaf Pan	8×4×3	1.5 L	20×10×7
	9×5×3	2 L	23×13×7
Round Layer Cake Pan	8×1½	1.2 L	20×4
	9×1½	1.5 L	23×4
Pie Plate	8×1¼	750 mL	20×3
	9×1¼	1 L	23×3
Baking Dish or Casserole	1 quart	1 L	—
	1½ quarts	1.5 L	—
	2 quarts	2 L	—